FITTING IN AFTER FIFTY
To Your New Town

ELAINE L. ORR

Copyright © 2019 Elaine L. Orr

All rights reserved.

Library of Congress Control Number: 2019908847
ISBN-13: 978-1-948070-33-1

DEDICATION

To adventurous folks willing to

try new places and

new things.

ACKNOWLEDGMENTS

Thanks to the Decatur, Illinois "Write Stuff" Critique Group, whose members are generous with their time and tough with their comments.

CHAPTER ONE

Reasons for the Move and Getting Started

Attitudes toward a move vary by why it's occurring. They'll be different if you've built a dream home in a warmer climate than if you lost a job and have to move hundreds of miles for a new one. Maybe you're moving to be closer to frail family members or to spend time with grandchildren.

Are you going back to a place you've lived before? If you've visited through the years, changes could have seemed gradual. If you're a military family that decided to return to your favorite residence (and haven't been there in years) you may be surprised at a town's evolution.

Harder may be moving as a spouse when the two of you had no plans to do so. Even if your spouse would also have preferred to stay where you were, as the trailing spouse, life can feel out of control.

Whatever the reason for the uprooting, you will find good things about your new community and good people who live there.

LEARNING FROM A DISTANCE

Likely you won't pack your bags two weeks after making the decision to relocate. There are helpful approaches to getting to know the new town. What can you do from a distance?

- Read the local paper online and consider a hard-copy subscription for a month. Much may not be included in the online edition.

- Instill a sense of place through maps (not just digital versions). A map can also help younger kids or grandkids get a sense of your new location. In relation to them, of course.

- Check out the town or county's website. There are usually links to community organizations and events.

- Even if you aren't buying, seek out house or apartment guides. They can tell you a lot about neighborhoods. A realtor may be willing to mail them to you, figuring that you could be a client one day.

- If you plan to rent before you buy, consider renting a post office box for a time. It can save you from having to quickly change your address again if you move within your new community.

- Research local storage units, especially if you are moving to a smaller place. You may think you've gotten rid of everything you don't need, but it's almost a certainty that the closets and attic at the new place won't hold what you think. (And if it doesn't fit, ask yourself why you have it.)

- Learn who the employers are. Your new neighbors will tell you where they work, and it would be good to respond with an expression other than a blank stare. Though you certainly can – no one will expect you to know the terrain.

- Call the Chamber of Commerce to see if they have a welcome packet or know an organization that prepares them.

- Gather information about a town's history. It can tell you a lot about the current culture of the place. Wikipedia will have some, but you may also find local pictorial history books by Arcadia Publishing or online versions of older books about a city or county. Visit the local historical society after you arrive.

The library is a crucial resource. They may have books or pamphlets to help you know the area. More important, librarians have been asked every possible question about the town, and they know how to find answers. Some libraries have small staffs, so ask if it's a good time to talk, or if you should pose your question and call back.

As you do your research, make lists of information or what you plan to do because you learned it. If you don't write down the storage unit's phone number, you'll have to hunt again.

In learning about a town or making the move, one technique is especially helpful.

Make to-do lists. And then follow through.

MAKING THE MOVE

This book is not a moving guide – you can get lists of tasks online or from a moving company. However, this compilation of ideas will give you food for thought.

- Does your bank have a branch in the new town? If not, do you want to open an account when you do an apartment or house-hunting trip? Many banks now let you open accounts online. (This may require a post office box if you don't yet have a local address and want one on your checks.)

- Compare the cost of using a moving company with those of a self-move. You may be surprised that there is not too much difference, because you pay a mileage fee for a U-Haul or Penske truck. Moving companies will give estimates based on number of rooms or pounds of goods. Remember, the more unused stuff you get rid of, the cheaper the move.

- Hint: Consider buying insurance, especially if you are renting a truck yourself. I don't buy insurance when I rent a car for a few days, but always do for a move. If there is any kind of accident, your car insurance may cover the moving van, but you would cover the income the rental company lost because it was out of service. I speak from experience. We once pulled a trailer during a move, and a car broke down immediately in front of us. I stopped the car fine, but the trailer, which had no brakes, slammed into the car. Having the insurance from the rental company simplified everything. If you use a mover, insure your contents for more than the relatively small amount the mover may provide.

- Rummage/Garage sales are a lot of work, but getting rid of some 'stuff' could fund the move. You can also sell through local Facebook groups or (for easy-to-mail items) eBay. Be sure to carefully read a site's guidance. If you sell locally and will meet to exchange the item for cash, do it in the daytime and in a public place. A lot of police stations permit you to use their lobbies.

- Contact utility and cable companies in both locations. Your current one will forward the final bill to your new address.

- Cable or dish companies may have lead times of a week or more. You can buy a converter box online for about $30. This lets you pick up over-the-air channels and could buy you hours of peace and quiet if you have kids. You'll need an inexpensive indoor antenna. Not too many stores sell the boxes, and they can be more expensive than online.

- Boxes and packing tape will be your new best friends. If you collect some from stores, avoid any that have held fresh food. Consider spraying (outside) the bottom of store boxes with bug spray. Walmart has inexpensive brown moving boxes in the office supply aisle, and U-Haul boxes are competitively priced. If you need a lot, you can buy boxes in bulk online. You have to pack your sheets and towels, so employ some to wrap dishes. I use a lot of paper towels because I can re-use them to wipe up spills at the new place. Plastic bags from the grocery store also make good packing material (if they have not held fresh food or meat).

- Collect medical records from current doctors and dentists, including digital copies of x-rays or other tests. Write a concise medical history of yourself and family members. I suggest putting it in the car's glove box. When you are in a new doctor's office, they want a history. You'll forget a lot.

- Finding new doctors is hard, and some may be closed to new patients. Most hospitals have info on doctors who will take new patients. Check to be sure they accept your insurance. It's okay to look at doctor ratings online, but keep in mind that people who post may lean toward those who are displeased about some aspect of their treatment. Sometimes they are unhappy because of their illness or pain more than because of what the doctor did (or could not do) about it. Neighbors or realtors may have suggestions.

- Don't try to unpack everything in two days. Yes, an orderly residence is comforting, but an injured back means discomfort for weeks or months. You need a bed, bedding, towels, a few items of clothing, medicine and toiletries. You only need enough kitchen items to warm soup, make coffee, and store leftovers from take-out meals. A good book and wine round out the necessities.

You can put your pile of empty boxes at the curb on a sunny day to see if anyone wants them, or place an ad on Freecycle or Craigslist.

Ultimately, you'll be done. Since you were so busy with the logistics of move, the quiet can be almost disconcerting. Other parts of this book provide ideas to fill the quiet time.

RESOURCES FOR CHAPTER ONE
Reasons Why and Getting Started

Most resources are web-based, so that you can easily find them. You can also do your own web search for topics such as "moving to ABC city, state."

Why do you see the full web link? Sometimes an electronic book or article may react differently to short links, or you may be reading a paperback. If you have to type in the link, try doing just the first part (through dot com or dot org). Then you can search for the article.

Where Should I Live? 14 Important Factors When Deciding the Best Place to Live.

While the premise in this book is that you've made the move decision, there are a lot of interesting questions and links in this article – including those to *Kiplinger's* and *Money Magazine's* best places to live.

https://www.moneycrashers.com/where-should-i-live-decide-best-places/

Fourteen Things to Do When You Move to a New Town.
Wisebread is a website for Living Large on a Small Budget
https://www.wisebread.com/14-things-you-should-do-when-you-move-to-a-new-town

How to Prevent Loneliness When Moving to a New Town.
This website is geared more toward moving than settling in, but you can find resources for both.
https://www.unpakt.com/blog/prevent-loneliness-moving-new-town/

On Retirement: Apartment Living Can be the Right Choice, Evadna Bartlett, *Gazette-Mail,* April 19, 2016.
https://www.wvgazettemail.com/life/on-retirement-apartment-living-can-be-the-right-choice/article_ad8c1b79-4485-507a-85c1-2e69b155ca4a.html

Moving from Big House to Small Apartment: How to Adjust, Ann Hoge on Bangitout Blog, July 11, 2017.
http://www.bangitout.com/placemarks/moving-from-big-house-to-small-apartment-how-to-adjust/

AARP has articles on almost every topic.

Downsizing? Ditch these Items, Jeff Yeager, AARP. This is a slide show, but it moves quickly and the pictures are useful.
https://www.aarp.org/money/budgeting-saving/info-2015/downsizing-items-to-ditch-photo.html#slide1

Differences Between Paper Maps and Digital Maps, Grind GIS
https://grindgis.com/maps/differences-between-paper-maps-and-digital-maps

Think you'll need a lot of paper maps or trip guides? It could be worth a year of AAA membership.
https://autoclubsouth.aaa.com/membership/aaa_membership_plans.aspxlant.

CHAPTER TWO

Deciding How Involved You Want to Be

I come from a family of very friendly people. We are also a mix of introverts and extroverts, and a person's approach to a new town will likely be based on that element of their personality.

However you approach breaking into a town, you'll have to take some action. When I moved to Iowa, a Welcome Wagon Woman was at my door within a relatively short time. She had information and small gifts from local business owners. The organization still exists as a way for businesses to advertise to new residents, but everything appears to be through print and digital advertising.

Some towns still have newcomer organizations. Check with the library. You can also Google a variation of "xyz town newcomer group" or "local newcomer organization." If your computer or phone allows location access, you may get links of nearby groups. I could find no central resource.

Basically, you're on your own, perhaps with the help of new neighbors. It's up to you to decide how involved you want to be in your new community. This could be a quieter time in your life and you'll be content to see what's on the newspaper's community calendar, get a library card, eat out with your spouse once a week, and occasionally see a movie. The rest of the time you'll be reading, gardening, or cruising social media to keep in touch with friends from other places.

On the other hand, this could be your time to thrive – your kids are independent (knock on wood) and you have been at the job long enough to have a more flexible schedule. Or you're retired.

This can be your time to develop a new group of acquaintances or friends so that each weekend (or several times each week) something is on your calendar. In the digital age, you can Google any topic to find a local element – bridge groups, photography clubs, softball or basketball leagues.

Bring it on!

PASSIVE VERSUS ACTIVE ENGAGEMENT

In a medium or larger city you can be around people without talking to anyone. Attend a movie, visit a museum, browse a book or sporting goods store, shop at the weekend farmers' market, eat at a mall food court – maybe even attend a professional sporting event.

Wherever you are you can take a walk in a park or around the block. Try not to look devious.

In a small town, there are far fewer passive ways to spend time. If you want to be around people – especially if you want to make friends – you have to attend activities or join organizations populated by like-minded people.

You'll need to think through broad parameters of how to spend your time. If you don't, you'll simply be reacting to invitations. And they usually do come, especially in smaller communities.

I was in my mid-forties when I first moved to Iowa – during a cold winter. I saw that a bank was having a New Year's Eve reception that would end about ten PM. There were also parties at a hotel, but those sounded like events to attend when you already knew people. I went to the bank and met some nice people. I had people to say hello to in the grocery store.

The following summer I had an individual friend, but still hadn't made a group of friends. I like groups, so I kept introducing myself to people. At a lunch-in-the-park event I moved from table to table saying hello and introducing myself. People were polite, but they definitely thought I was weird.

At the last table, an older woman said, "Did you graduate from college?" My first thought was "how rude," but I said yes. She said, "Good. You're coming to AAUW Travel Club pot-luck dinner with me Monday night."

AAUW is the American Association of University Women. It was founded at a time when women weren't allowed in most professional organizations, and members focus a lot on education opportunities for girls. I'd found my niche and had a dozen friends within a few months. I would not have expected to find close friends in a professional group, and if I hadn't been table-hopping in the park I would not have.

Later I joined the Lions Club and met dozens of people who like to have fun and help kids with vision problems. You may find your friends by joining a mixed league at the bowling alley, taking an exercise class at a gym, or going to a program at the library.

Remember, you don't meet anyone until you ditch the remote and get off the couch.

DECIDING WHAT TO DO WITH WHOM

You aren't obligated to accept offers to participate, but you may need to develop criteria for declining them. Sometimes it's easy. You can say you don't like to visit community pools because you sunburn easily. That doesn't have to be true. You should simply be able to say no thank you to such invitations, but some people push – they think they are being nice. White lies can be handy.

When you live alone, you can make your own list of the kinds of activities to participate in, and whether they can be done alone or with others. Some may be similar to hobbies or functions from your prior locale, others could be completely different. Why not try something new in a new place?

If you have a partner or spouse, you'll have to determine how much you want to do alone or together. You may have very different goals for interaction at this point in your lives, and you don't need to do everything together.

If your partner or spouse thinks you should always accompany each other, talk about it. If they persist in wanting constant companionship, it could be their own shyness or their way of controlling your actions. You may need informal counseling with friends or family, or professional advice. What you do should be up to you.

That said, be realistic in deciding what you can or are able to do. The senior softball league may sound like fun, but when is the last time you ran at sprint speed?

GETTING WHERE YOU WANT TO GO

Access can make a difference in what you choose to do.

Do you have transportation to get where you want to go, or do you need to research public transportation or set up an Uber account? A local senior center can tell you if there is door-to-door pick-up for people with limited mobility.

Think about driving in a new place. Perhaps it's just a matter of learning new routes, or maybe the volume of traffic or types of roads are very different than where you used to live.

I lived in the DC metro area, and the town itself is on a grid. You always knew where North-South-East-West were. Mostly you'd give directions by saying things such as, "If you're going toward the Smithsonian, go south on 19th Street and turn left on Constitution."

In a town of 25,000 in Iowa, some directions were given that way. More often someone would say, "Go to Second Street and head west." It was years before such directions became intuitive for me. And it took practice.

Get a paper map. Google Maps and Map Quest are great, but you see things in chunks and it's hard to get a perspective of your town or county. You also need an Internet connection. If you belong to AAA, maps are free, but you can get free them at highway rest stops or state transportation departments. Local visitor centers and Chambers of Commerce often have city or county maps, as do most car and truck rental offices.

As much as I love paper maps, I use Google Maps locally all the time. Digital maps are a wonderful reference in a new town, and having the Apps on a phone literally puts them at your fingerprints.

You can also email or text directions to yourself. I recommend texting because sometimes you can access your texts when you can't get Internet on your phone.

Definitely look up where you're going before you rely only on a GPS system. I once followed directions that led me along a dirt road that was almost a cow path. Less than a quarter-mile away was a 'real' road. Google did thank me for sending the feedback.

RESOURCES FOR CHAPTER TWO
Deciding How Involved You Want to Be

Deciding how involved to be is not something most people usually do consciously. Each of these resources may help you think through some aspects of the issue.

You may need to simply know what's available before you can decide how to be involved. You can start with local guidebooks, but also search for topics such as "what to do this weekend in xyx." Below is Iowa's answer to that question, organized by town and topic.
https://www.traveliowa.com/calendar/

10 Questions that Will Help You Decide What to Do in Retirement, Joe Hearn, Lifestyle Design
https://intentionalretirement.com/2013/11/what-to-do-during-retirement/

How to Start Over in a New City: Six Lessons I learned the Hard Way, Winona Dimeo-Ediger
Rather than where or how to move, this Livability article asks the question, "Once you've moved to a new place, how do you adjust and thrive?"
https://livability.com/topics/make-your-move/how-to-start-over-in-a-new-city-6-lessons-i-learned-the-hard-way

CHAPTER THREE

Getting to Know the Immediate Neighborhood or Complex

Getting to know the neighbors takes skill. You want to be reasonably friendly, but if someone is loud or complains a lot, you won't want to spend much time with them. You mostly don't want them to take offense if you decline invitations – unless they are really obnoxious, then you won't care too much.

This chapter discusses getting to know people who live near you, with occasional tips for how to remain aloof. It is organized by type of residence, but some actions are good whether you're in a home or apartment.

- Smile and nod. That gives others an opening, should they want to engage.

- Be willing to introduce yourself and stick out your hand, but don't be offended if your actions are barely (or not at all) reciprocated.

- Attend announced events, such as block parties, as well as informal activities, such as rummage sales.

- Buy what local kids sell – within reason. Some schools still raise money through direct sales (think cookie dough and wrapping paper), while Scouts now tend to set up at local shopping centers.

- Become aware of local sports teams—school and professional. Sport pride and the weather are neutral topics in grocery store lines, which is where you'll see your neighbors.

- Ask Suri or Alexa what's going on. I never thought I would talk to a round piece of plastic (I use Amazon's Alexa on an Echo Dot), but these devices (which require an internet connection) are handy for weather, local news, and activities. I also link Alexa to my Google calendar, and it gives me verbal reminders.

SAFETY FIRST

A realtor or apartment manager should be able to tell you if the area is safe to walk alone or after dark. Local police or a community association could have crime data by neighborhood. May it all be dull data.

If you have children or grandchildren, you want to revisit the stranger danger conversation. Where you used to live, talking to neighbors (whom you knew) was okay, unless you said otherwise.

In a new place, you don't want kids being friendly with just anyone who walks up and says they're grandma's neighbor. It's such a balancing act. You won't leave young children alone in the yard or driveway. But you could turn your back for a second, and harm can happen fast.

The other big safety topic is swimming pools. The apartment complex may have one, or neighbors may have a private pool. In a warm climate, your own home could have one. Curious kids or babies can drown in a minute. Same goes for hot tubs. Make sure locks are strong and fencing is in place.

These are not pleasant thoughts. Because your mind may be on unpacking (or anything else), it never hurts to be reminded to be aware.

IF YOU LIVE IN A HOUSE

In some neighborhoods, people will introduce themselves, in others you could live there a year and rarely speak. The latter seems (to me) to be more characteristic of suburbs in which most residents work, or if the street has a lot of traffic.

One couple I knew met few people, so they invited small groups of neighbors to dinner. Some had lived near each other for years but never met. Dinner seems like a big commitment of time and money, but maybe a couple of coffee and pastry events could bring people together.

You could move into a neighborhood like ours in Illinois, which has two annual neighborhood-wide garage sales and a Facebook page. They even welcome people who live in the apartments. It's not as if everyone in the hundreds of homes knows one another, but you feel a sense of connection.

It's easy to start a Facebook page for your vicinity. Better, perhaps, if one already exists, but at least you can start the connection.

APARTMENT COMPLEXES

In an apartment (especially one you enter through an interior hallway) you'll readily see neighbors. Some will say hello, a few will recognize you as new and introduce themselves. Others will keep their eyes down because they don't want to meet people. That's okay, too.

Inside mailboxes are a great place to introduce yourself to other residents, though they could be preoccupied with the mail or dinner on the stove. Think about some scenes from *The Big Bang Theory*.

Any garden apartments or townhomes built in the last fifty years have groups of mailboxes, as do some newer single-family neighborhoods. People tend to drive up, hop out, and grab mail, especially in the winter. In warmer weather you could strike up a conversation.

Senior apartment complexes are discussed later in this chapter. Even in 'all age' apartments there could be common areas such as pools or a community room. If there is not a monthly coffee for new neighbors in the community room, the manager might be willing to offer one – as long as they don't have to do all the work.

In apartments or townhomes, you'll share a parking lot or garage. Make sure you obey all parking rules! Tell visitors to not to park in numbered spaces – numbers always mean the space has been assigned.

LIVING IN A SENIOR COMMUNITY

Most places I've lived have (private) senior complexes and offer continuing care communities. You can move from independent homes or apartments to assisted living to nursing home care.

A lot of towns also have apartments for seniors on more limited incomes. These are not necessarily public housing, but may have been built with special financing and are managed by nonprofit groups.

Senior complexes often have activities or places to drink coffee. In one Maryland building my father lived in, they had an ongoing rummage sale of sorts in the basement coffee area; he regularly checked it out. Candidly, many of the goods came when residents died and their families donated apartment contents. We did.

Senior residences may have a shared (informal) library or game room. Organized activities may be more regular. Don't let anyone goad you into the morning exercise class, but it could be fun.

In his senior apartment, my father was very sociable, and even joined a singing group and played Santa for kids' groups with some other residents. In a nursing home, our mom could not really socialize. She was friendly with a couple other residents and the staff arranged for talking books. She enjoyed her privacy. My mother-in-law was in a lovely assisted living apartment for years. She didn't participate in a lot of activities but loved bingo and probably read every book in the place and, later, in the complex's nursing home.

If you have several options in your town, find out what others think of a building or facility, but investigate yourself. One person may say "there's nothing to do" but you'll like the activities. Another may say (for assisted living or independent living with a lunch meal) that the food isn't good. Most places that require that you eat there have alternate menus if you don't like the main course.

To me, the best thing about senior communities is avoidance of isolation. You're not only around other people regularly, there can be transportation to shopping, social events, or church.

You need to be prepared to assert yourself if needed. Some places seat you at lunch tables with people you don't know and expect you to eat meals with them for years. If you have friends in the same building and want to eat together, say you'd like to. If you are refused, ask to be served in your apartments and eat together that way.

After a while the host organization may tire of bringing you meals and let you sit with friends. If you handle everything politely, you'll get what you feel you need. Remember, you're paying for the services you receive.

AVOIDING FOUR-LEGGED FRUSTRATIONS

After getting engaged, a friend began walking her fiancé's dogs. She said if she'd known how easy it was to meet people she would have bought a dog years earlier.

Make sure you know the local rules for pets. Leash laws? Probably – even for cats. What happens if your dog gets out and is picked up the local animal control? How do you retrieve them?

We do a well visit at a local vet almost immediately. You never know when you'll need a quick appointment. Larger towns may have an emergency vet open at night, but those are more expensive.

Pets are great, but they can lead to neighborhood discord. Let your dog poop on someone else's lawn and your first conversation with a neighbor may be strained. We lived on a corner lot in Iowa, and at a spot near the street I had to clean poop a lot.

Humor helps, I had a sign made.

Doggies are nice, but not their poop.
If you walk your dog, carry a scoop.

No more little gifts. When we got ready to move, people asked if they could have the sign! I had ordered two, figuring one could get taken (it didn't), so I was able to accommodate two neighbors.

We have two cats, and when we move to a new place I walk them on leashes until they know the area. They were shelter cats and had been in cages quite a while, so they were pretty docile. Other cats we've had would never have permitted such an indignity. The cats now trail us on walks, no leashes needed. I meet a lot of apartment neighbors while walking those cats.

Cats can be as unpopular as roaming dogs. They kill birds and bunnies, and one of ours was apparently good at it. She didn't bring a lot home, so I didn't realize the full extent of her accomplishments.

When we lived in a house in Indiana, a man who lived around the corner came over and yelled at my husband one Sunday morning. All he had to do was say he didn't want the cat near his bird feeder. We promptly bought a mesh pet tent (which we called kitty prison) and tied a long leash to a tree during the day.

The cats are now 15 and sit on the front porch of the apartment we live in in Illinois. Also the neighbor's porch, but he doesn't mind. They still like walks and even let neighbors pet them.

Bottom line, if you have pets, talk to your neighbors. Let them know you'll control your pet, and that they're vaccinated.

RESOURCES FOR CHAPTER THREE
Getting to Know the Immediate Neighborhood or Complex

How Safe is Your Neighborhood? Use these 5 Tools to Find Out. Alexia Chianis on the Safewise blog.
https://www.safewise.com/blog/confirm-safety-neighboorhood-online-tools/

3 Ways to Learn Your New Neighborhood. BlestOxy Blog, August 31, 2017
http://www.blestoxy.com/2017/08/31/3-ways-to-learn-your-new-neighborhood/

Discover Your Neighborhood
The NextDoor site can lead you to your neighbors. Put in your address and see if there is a local website for your area. My Illinois neighborhood has one and I love it.
https://nextdoor.com/find-neighborhood/

And leave it to AARP
Social Etiquette Tips for Using NextDoor, Lexi Pandell, *AARP The Magazine*, May 31, 2018
https://www.aarp.org/home-family/personal-technology/info-2018/nextdoor-app.html

Register with entities to form or join a group

Google, and Facebook require you to register with them to join or participate in any group. You have to be in FB to use its groups. The email you use to be a member of a Google group does not have to be a Google email address.

Join or Create a Facebook Group
Join as few or as many if you want. If you don't want to see announcement of who posted what, turn off notifications. Search first by your town or neighborhood.
https://www.facebook.com/groups

Join or Create a Google Group
Overview of Google Groups
https://groups.google.com/forum/#!overview

How to Create a Google Group, a wikiHow article
https://www.wikihow.com/Create-a-Google-Group

Getting Pets Acclimated
Moving House, Settling Your Cat Into a New House, VetWest Animal Hospital
https://www.vetwest.com.au/pet-library/moving-house-settling-your-cat-into-a-new-house

7 Ways to Help Dogs and Cats Adjust to a New Home, Certa Pet, May 8, 2018
https://www.certapet.com/cats-and-dogs-new-home/

CHAPTER FOUR
Beyond Your Street or Building

When we first moved to Indiana, my husband suggested I not find a traditional job, but instead try to publish some of the books I'd written. I did, and had some success. Yea!

But, we lived in an apartment and I was initially alone a lot. I wrote in a defunct coffee shop called the Left Bank, and a sign in the store became the name of the coffee shop in my Jolie Gentil series – Java Jolt.

I discussed with a physical therapist how hard it was to break into a community after age 60, and he used a phrase I've employed often – "You may have to look hard to find your tribe, but it's there."

Where to look for yours?

- Coffee shop. They offer something to do when you know no one, and it's okay if you sit for a couple of hours. I visited a Starbucks when we first moved to Illinois (no Internet for a time) and ended up going there to write up to five times a week. I knew all the regulars and ended up dedicating a book to the staff.

- Local senior center. Almost every town of a few thousand people has one. It may be an older group of seniors, but they're nice people. Sometimes there are bridge or chess groups and other activities. The staff or volunteers know local resources for seniors, especially help with transportation.

- Community colleges. Many have free classes for people over a certain age (60 in Maryland, 65 in Illinois). Community colleges may offer free concerts or moderately-priced plays. Take a French class and meet someone to travel to Paris with.

- Churches. The denomination that you belonged to may not be there, or may not be as friendly as your prior church. It's okay to "church shop" when you get to a new place. In Illinois, my church has also become my social activity hub.

- Hobby groups. There are groups for everything: dancing, running, gardening, family history, photography, kayaking, senior sports teams, yoga, stargazing, chess, bridge, backgammon, and more. Local papers usually list community activities at least weekly, or ask at the library.

- YMCA or health club classes. You may need to join, but most give out week-long passes. If they don't, tell them they should and you could be the first.

- Library book groups or classes. I've lived in towns where all kinds of events run out of the library, and some where things pretty much relate to reading. One where I now live has a huge children's play area, and a lot of grandparents bring their grandkids to play. Volunteer to work at the annual book sale.

- Veterans groups. You can only join if you are a vet, but they may have barbeques or special events. If you feel a close kinship with veterans but are not one yourself, some have auxiliary organizations that others can join.

- Community groups with regular meals. The Knights of Columbus in one Iowa town has a Friday Fish Fry. Lots of service groups have pancake breakfasts throughout the year.

- Service Groups. If you really want to get involved in a town, join Lions, Rotary, Kiwanis, Elks or a similar group. Go to a meeting as a guest and make it clear you are visiting all of them, so you don't get too much pressure to join one immediately. Each has their own culture and groups for which they raise funds.

- Business groups or locally owned stores. Introduce yourself and get on their mailing lists for special events. These are more prominent in the Midwest and smaller communities than in big cities.

Look for periodic newspaper supplements geared to hobbies, holidays, festivals, or senior citizens.

May is Older Americans Month – every paper in the country does at least some features along this theme. Why? Because seniors spend money, so the paper can get advertisers. Same for the periodic newsletters.

SOCIAL MEDIAL RESOURCES AND NETWORKING

Anything here will be outdated in a year, but this discussion can be a starting point. You don't need to do anything with social media, but it's hard to imagine learning a new environment without it. I suppose you could pull out a phone book, if they are still distributed in your town.

Head first to Facebook and put in the name of your town and the state, and see what pops up. The town and county Facebook pages will likely be first, and this will take you to their official websites. Lots of links to resources there.

After government groups you'll find local businesses or prominent people, probably garage sale sites, and maybe pages that relate to other aspects of your life. If you've previously joined groups or liked pages that deal with pets, the local animal shelter may pop up. Click on that and you see they need volunteer dog walkers, and you have a chance to meet other dog lovers.

If you're a veteran, the local VFW or DAV chapters could appear, and if you belong to your prior church's Facebook group, that denomination's local church(es) could emerge. I've liked a few pages that related to illnesses that friends have, and local support groups pop up.

Next try Twitter. In the search box, put in the town or county, Some links to organizations will pop up, but you'll be more likely to find references to events or high school sports teams. Also people's opinions on goings-on in town. A lot of these will be positive. If they aren't, ignore the negative ones.

Twitter and Facebook can lead you to other websites.

After you've searched by location, look for Facebook groups that relate to your hobbies, the schools in the town, or tourist attractions.

Why are you doing this? You'll see not only groups that could interest you, but also the people who post in them. I'm not one to ask strangers to be Facebook friends, but I periodically message someone I don't know to ask a question. If someone regularly posts in a Master Gardeners' Group, no reason you can't write to them to see if azaleas grow well in the region. When they respond, you'll know one more person.

The usual social media precautions apply. Don't agree to meet a stranger in an uncrowded place, and never talk about money. If you decide to go to a certain meeting or event, go with a friend or family member or post your schedule on your refrigerator.

ACT LIKE A TOURIST

When you move to a new town or region, take in the local sights. If nothing else, this will get you out of unpacking boxes for a few hours.

Every town has something to see, even if it's a small town that showcases only the county fair or local coffee shop. I've lived in the Washington, DC metro area (monuments and museums) and Springfield, Illinois (think Lincoln). Cities such as these will have dozens of places to visit.

Consider Pinterest for sightseeing. If you don't know the term, it's an image-based website. People organize images into boards (think bulletin boards).

These can be photos a person took themselves or images downloaded from elsewhere (if they aren't copyrighted or trademarked). You can also form your own boards. If you put in your new town's name, local venues will pop up.

It's easier to describe by example, so take a look at my Pinterest boards https://www.pinterest.com/elaineorr55/.

RESOURCES FOR CHAPTER FOUR
Beyond Your Street or Building

Chapter Three reference on Facebook, and Google Groups would apply here as well.

Do a Google or other search for your town, county, or region name and words such as tourism, visitor guide, places to visit. A lot will pop up.

Call the Office of the mayor, town manager, or county commissioner to inquire about local resources. These are not trip-planning or local events offices, but they may be able to guide you to local resources. So can their web pages. Search for "xxx website."

This Is Where You Belong: Finding Home Wherever You Are, Melody Warnick, Penguin Books, 2016 (Amazon has new and used copies, and a Kindle edition)

149 Best Hobbies for Men, Kyle Boureston on the Mantelligence Website
https://www.mantelligence.com/50-fun-hobbies-for-men/
What this article will give you is a sense of what can be found in many places. Personally, I don't know about the spearfishing, but you'll find many suggested ways to meet people. Also lots of ideas for things you can do alone.

Senior Resources Blog. Informative articles about twice per week. Some deal with activities, some with

different interests. The site is sponsored by a senior living organization.
https://bonaventuresenior.com/blog/

Links through the American Association of Retired Persons
Visit AARP's website for your state. Sometimes there are articles about your part of the state, mostly links to discussions that might interest older Americans in the state, or policy issues AARP has taken a stand on. For example:
https://states.aarp.org/maryland/
https://states.aarp.org/illinois

Lions Clubs International
www.lionsclubs.org/

Kiwanis International
www.kiwanis.org/

Rotary International
https://www.rotary.org/

List of Veterans Organizations
https://en.wikipedia.org/wiki/List_of_veterans%27_organizations

CHAPTER FIVE
Deciding Whether to Volunteer

In Chapter Four, I mentioned service clubs as a way to meet others. These people often have generous spirits.

The broader question of volunteering is an important one. Considerations include:

- How busy do you want to be?

- Can you afford to in effect work without pay?

- Do you want to volunteer regularly, or just occasionally?

- How good are you at protecting your time – essentially, saying no?

Groups that cater to children or families generally have younger volunteers. Soccer league parents staff concession booths and serve as chaperones for overnight trip. The same is true for class trips, swim meets, or scout camping. They may welcome older volunteers, but could have enough adults to go around.

For civic and community groups, the proportion of volunteers is often older, and includes a lot of retirees. But baby boomers (the largest named cohort) have aged, everyone works longer, and adults of all ages have more hobbies. There can be shortages of people who step forward to help.

The best example might be the cadre of dedicated folks to staff hospital volunteer desks. My observations say the largest proportion is in their late seventies or eighties.

While you will likely be welcome at any group you examine or join, you aren't obligated to sell raffle tickets or staff a booth at a bazaar simply because others say they need you to do that. I volunteer a lot. Many of my friends do. But I don't let myself get talked into anything. It's a good principle.

I divide volunteering into three categories:

- Events, such as a Race for the Cure or a neighborhood block party

- Ongoing activities, but still periodic, such as school tutoring, hospital helpers, or church fundraisers

- Leadership responsibilities, in which you provide guidance for others by chairing a group or managing a set of activities

Because my writing career is busy and I live far from (and like to visit) family and friends, I try largely for event-based activities. I do a couple ongoing activities (held only a couple of times per year).

I undertook leadership roles in various professional groups and nonprofits before 'retirement,' but I'm not willing to organize my time around such activities. Plus, I feel guilty when I fall behind because of my writing. I am historian for a large family reunion group, but that's also a lot of fun.

Fun is good. When you are devoted to a cause, you volunteer to provide a service and it may not be 'fun' per se. But the people you work with and what you accomplish should bring some joy. If not, consider whether your time can be used elsewhere.

THINGS TO VOLUNTEER FOR

If you don't see a way to break into the community, volunteering is it – within the parameters you set for yourself.

- Habitat for Humanity. If you have carpentry or any building trade skills (or even if you don't) see if there is a local Habitat for Humanity Chapter.

- Kids' sports leagues. Coach or get certified as a referee.

- County Fair Upkeep. Every county has fairgrounds and a group that oversees its operations. They always need volunteers to paint buildings, collect tickets, or work at a food booth.

- Hospitals. Some of these roles involve walking or pushing people in wheelchairs, but others require only sitting.

- Hospice. Many hospitals and nursing homes have hospice units, but there may also be a county or town organization that recruits volunteers for respite services or other duties.

- Local theater productions. You could take a hand at acting, paint scenery, or operate the concession stand.

- Boys and Girls Clubs and the YM or YWCAs have a myriad of activities, some during the school year, some in the summer.

- Local schools. Tutor, mentor, or help with sports teams. Check with the district office, as you usually need a background check.

- Senior Center. These may have some paid staff, but many tasks are performed by volunteers.

- Library. Read to kids, shelve books, host programs in keeping with your skills. (I do talks on writing or publishing.)

- Literacy programs. The schools or a library can tell you how to find them.

- Churches, temples, or mosques. Every religious group needs help with activities and programs. Once you get involved, you could be asked to do a lot, especially if you're willing to cook!

WHAT TO WATCH OUT FOR

Any organization of more than five people can have competing interests. That's fine. When you are the new kid on the block, there might be someone who wants to tell you what they don't like about an individual or get you "on their side" of an issue.

I use two lines. 1) I don't gossip and this sounds like gossip. 2) Since we're talking about XYZ, perhaps you'd want to draw them into this conversation.

That's not to say you shouldn't want to know how an organization works, and you could be getting some good advice – such as a particular volunteer's strong point is managing finances, but that person may not be who you want running the publicity campaign.

You'll be able to differentiate between info and innuendo. Once others know you can, you won't be pestered by blather.

If there seems to be a lot of infighting (which I find rare), you can bow out gracefully and pick another organization to which to donate your time.

RESOURCES FOR CHAPTER FIVE
Deciding Whether to Volunteer or Work

Guide to Volunteering, on the Charity Navigator website.
http://bit.ly/2XsuzEe

How to find a Volunteer Gig You'll Actually Enjoy, Thorin Klosowski on Life Hacker, 2012
https://lifehacker.com/how-to-find-a-volunteer-gig-youll-actually-enjoy-5938432

AARP's Volunteer Opportunity Board
https://www.aarp.org/giving-back/

How To Decide The Volunteering Organization You Want To Work With, Volunteering Solutions. This article and website deal with volunteering abroad. Retirees may be interested, even if it is not in your town.
https://www.volunteeringsolutions.com/blog/tips-for-deciding-volunteering-organization/

CHAPTER SIX
Making Friends or Dating in a New Place

Some of the most popular television shows feature groups of people who support one another and joke around – *Cheers, Big Bang Theory, Seinfeld, and...Friends*. We do like to hang out where everyone knows our name.

Previous chapters discussed getting to know neighbors and others in our community. Some of these people could become friends, but finding friends takes dedicated effort. You also don't want to look like you *need* friends. Nothing is more likely to send people running.

Dating is even trickier. There is the tension of one of you being interested in the other with the feeling not being mutual. And who makes the first move? And who pays? Don't you have enough to navigate in a new place without such decisions?

FRIENDS FIRST

Graduating seniors hear the expression, "Choose a job you love and you will never have to work a day in your life." The quote is often attributed to the Chinese sage, Confucius.

A friendship corollary would be, "Choose activities you love and you will always spend time with people you like."

I endorse both sayings, but neither one just happens. You prepare for a career field or at the very least have a set of criteria for the kind of job you'd like. You also have to do some research to know where to go to meet the kind of people you'd like to spend time with.

If you are single or your spouse is too incapacitated to go out much or at all, you'll be on your own. My mom had multiple sclerosis (MS) and strokes. No one thought of her as disabled; she was funny, smart, and well-read -- the center of much of what we did.

But she had to stop playing bridge or doing much of anything beyond family activities. Dad played golf, conned some people into playing his wild style of bridge, had morning coffee in his senior citizens' building, and visited family around the country. He also visited the nursing home five or six days a week once Mom had to enter one.

People understand why the spouse of an ill

person goes out alone. More difficult is if one spouse is comfortable in a new place and content to spend time at home, and the other wants to make new friends. A recently-retired spouse may have no intention of setting up a social calendar.

Separate activities are great when you both agree on that point. We discussed this in Chapter Two. If a spouse wants you nearby, you'll need to assert yourself about going out alone, or ask family members to help you make your point.

So what should you think about when looking for friends?

- Consider things that can be done with more than one person. Reading is solitary, but libraries have book clubs. Chess and backgammon require only one partner, and many towns have clubs. Make sure a bridge group plays for fun and no one screams if you bid incorrectly. ☺

- Select activities where you mingle with others. If you attend a talk, you interact only with the people near you. Or attend a talk with a social hour afterwards.

- Take your own car or arrange independent transportation – at least until you know the setting and people.

- Find a church, meditation, or yoga group. Make it clear you are visiting several similar entities. Go as often as you like, but don't create a commitment until you are certain you'll want to spend time with members of the group.

- Join sponsored day trips or weekend tours. Some are commercial, others are sponsored by local media groups, churches, banks, or clubs.

- Check out the online media calendars (radio, TV, newspapers). I've lived in towns with National Public Radio (NPR) stations, and they sponsor (often with other community groups) several activities a year. I don't drink, but if you like wine you'll especially enjoy these events.

Some people shy away from activities that involve families with children, but I like to be around younger people. I'm not talking about hanging out at the kiddie pool in the summer (though community pools are a great way to meet people); more like joining the high school booster club. I get involved with youth activities in my church, not teaching on Sunday, but some of the social events and camps.

POSSIBLY THE BEST ADVICE

In an article on the *Business Insider* website (see the Resources section), Ellen Hendriksen discussed the importance of seeing the same people regularly. She suggests you stand less of a chance of making a friend at a mix-and-mingle type event than at a consistent activity.

Hendriksen says, "...think about how to see the same people on a regular basis. Rule out drop-ins, like one-time meetups or special events, and look for activities where the same core people show up every day or every week, like going to the local dog park, choral group practice, Thursday night running group, or anywhere you can be a 'regular.'"

I believe this, too. Remember, it wasn't until I started regularly going to AAUW events in Iowa that I felt I had a core group of friends. And I met someone who invited me because I went, alone, to the Friday lunch-in-the park event in my town and introduced myself to people. (Remember, too, I said some of them clearly thought I was odd. Who cares?)

If you aren't that bold, think about library book clubs – no membership fees and you can come and go from month to month.

THE DATING ROUTINE

Sometimes the hardest part is figuring out who's available to date. I cannot count the number of times people have assumed that because I went somewhere alone I was looking for a date. A few times men even acted offended that I didn't wear a sign saying 'unavailable' or 'uninterested.' I think it's an ego thing.

My husband is quieter, so I do a lot on my own. Because of some joint problems I can't wear a wedding ring. I used to wear something around my neck, and then I decided I didn't owe anyone an advertisement or explanation of my marital status.

If you do want to make your status known (and it can be easier sometimes), mention a boyfriend, girlfriend, or spouse. Among a group of strangers, you don't have to be precise with terminology to make your point. The same references work for opposite-sex or same-sex partners.

You can be clear, but someone else could be less than direct. Personally, I think the biggest hint that the "I just want to be friends" person wants more is if they want to do things alone with you. I don't mean alone in a dark alley; it can be a movie or coffee.

That's not to say you won't make close platonic

friends with people who are also dating candidates. I've spent as much of my adult life single as married, so I have lots of such friends. Usually I met them through mutual friends or in a group, and we found hobbies or interests in common. That's the way it is with all friends.

STARTING WITH AN ONLINE MATCH

When I was single in the 1980s, local papers or magazines had ISO ads – In Search Of [someone to date]. The *Washingtonian Magazine* would almost fly off some shelves each month. Remember, no Internet.

Online dating no longer has a stigma attached. I literally cannot count the friends who have made local connections through Match.com. To a person, they say it's easier to get the "what have you done with your life" discussion up front. And of course you can filter potential partners by interests, age, and lots of other factors.

You can check out a person's on-line presence via Facebook, LinkedIn and other social media sites. You can also check online criminal records. None of this helps if the person is good at deception, which is why you should always meet in a public place, preferably with a friend nearby. Never (and I do mean never) get in a car with someone you've just met, no matter how friendly.

Check out the online safety tips in the Resources section of this chapter. You can apply many of the concepts to in-person dating with people you've just met.

DON'T GET DISCOURAGED

You probably won't make new friends in a week. In fact, if you set a timetable, I can almost guarantee you won't meet it.

However, if you keep at least a couple of activities on your calendar every week, you'll enjoy being busy with people who have similar interests.

I'll tell you part of my story, which relates to friends and dating.

When I moved to Iowa in my mid-forties, I figured I would remain single. I wasn't looking to date, had tons of friends all over the country, was close to my family, and had taken my most serious steps toward a full-time writing career.

I'd been in the state about six weeks when the local paper advertised a writers' group at the library. I went, and the man who sat next to me on that frigid evening became my husband a few years later. Plus, I'm still friends with others I met that night.

Now, many of the people I socialize with I've met through my later-in-life writing career. So, you never know...

RESOURCES FOR CHAPTER SIX
Making Friends or Dating in a New Place

Many resources in Chapters Three and Four apply to making friends. Topics such as "making friends as an adult" or "making friends after forty" are popular for magazine web articles. Do a search and you'll find many.

Groupon has links to numerous activities. Go to the site and put in your zip code, or search by an interest. The example here is for bus tours.
https://www.groupon.com/local/bus-tours

How to Make Friends as an Adult, Danielle Page for NBC News, March 29, 2018
https://www.nbcnews.com/better/health/how-make-friends-adult-ncna860971

Research shows friend groups shrink after age 25. Here's how to keep making new friends even as you get older. Ellen Hendriksen, as a contributor to *Business Insider,* January 1, 2019

Making Friends When You're Married (Or in an Equivalent Long-Term Relationship), on the website Succeed Socially, undated
https://www.succeedsocially.com/howtomakefriendsmarried

Why Are We so Obsessed with Making Couple Friends? Rachel Raczka, *Washington Post*, May 13, 2018
https://www.washingtonpost.com/news/soloish/wp/2018/03/13/why-are-we-so-obsessed-with-having-couple-friends/

Online Dating Safety Tips: 14 Tips That Help You Have Fun and Stay Safe, Brianna Jensen on A Secure Life. 2018
hjttps://www.asecurelife.com/online-security/online-dating-safety/

If You're Dating in a New City, elite daily blog, Elana Rubin, May 30 2018
https://www.elitedaily.com/p/if-youre-dating-in-a-new-city-here-are-5-ways-to-make-it-easier-9170482

CHAPTER SEVEN
Holidays: Do You Stay or Do You Go?

Holidays or birthdays can be the hardest time in a new locale. If you had fun traditions with your family or friends elsewhere, you miss them. If you didn't, you may have high expectations for your new place. Those may have come to fruition, or they are (as yet) unfulfilled.

In a larger city – especially one like Washington, DC where people move in and out a lot – friends become family. Smaller towns, too, but not as much.

Unless you are within an easy drive of longtime connections (up to 250 miles for me), you have to factor in travel. Having Thanksgiving dinner can take time on both ends, plus the chance of being snowbound on the road or stuck in an airport. And it can be expensive.

Let's assume you are going to holiday in place. We'll think first of the secular aspects of holidays.

MAJOR HOLIDAYS

Always check media community calendars. If you don't subscribe to a paper, buy it the day or weekend prior to a holiday. If you aren't sure of the best day, call them. They can tell you when they feature holiday events in print. They'll be on the website, but sometimes print is more fun.

Valentine's Day. You may need to rely on sending cards and enjoying those you receive in return. (Send yours early.) Communities used to have sweetheart dances and things like that, but you don't see as much of these much. Keep an eye on local media calendars. If you've made a few friends and want to be silly, have a cookie-decorating party or play a sappy movie and chug (soft drinks or other) or eat heart-shaped chocolate when people kiss on screen.

St. Patrick's Day. Parades are popular in cities with a lot of Irish ancestors, such as New York and Chicago. In almost every town I've lived in, people have used St. Patrick's as a reason for a party. You may even see ads for parties, but usually these are at clubs or organizations where people know one another. And there is often a lot of drinking. Maybe okay with friends, boring as all get-out with strangers.

Memorial Day. Every local cemetery has Memorial Day events for deceased service members. Though not meant to be fun, they provide a sense of solidarity with neighbors. If you join a community pool, Memorial Day weekend is usually the start of the season. In smaller towns there could be block parties or a service club may have a barbeque or pancake breakfast.

Fourth of July. Parades and fireworks. Parades are sometimes followed by a community picnic and games. Some really small towns may have fireworks on a different day, since it's much cheaper to get professional companies on days other than the 4th. Please don't let anyone talk you into lighting anything yourself. Indiana was a culture shock for me because citizens could buy really LOUD devices to set off anywhere around the 4th.

Labor Day. End-of-season picnics may pop up, but so will events celebrating labor unions' role in building America. Typically it's the unions or the local Democrat party that sponsor these.

Halloween. Remember when this was a holiday for kids? The most fun would usually be costume parties with friends (hide the pictures). A number of communities have adult events, and schools or shopping malls may have indoor trick or treating. Volunteer to help at a children's party in the community.

Veterans' Day. While Veterans' organizations may sponsor serious or fun activities, it's also become popular for grocery stores, restaurants, or community venues to host breakfasts for vets. Some towns have parades or other civic events.

THANKSGIVING

This is still largely a U.S. holiday everyone celebrates. Religious or ethnic holidays may be appreciated by others, but Thanksgiving is a time for all.

Sadly, stores started opening on Thanksgiving in the 1970s. They think if they wait until late in the day they are respecting family time. The people who think this don't do the cooking or clean-up, and if they do some of it, they miss the point of simply relaxing with family and friends.

People may celebrate with the standard turkey and trimmings, and new recipes get introduced as our palettes broaden. If you invite friends over, see if they have a traditional dish that you don't. I'd never heard of green bean casserole for Thanksgiving, but it was a staple with my husband's family.

If you are on your own, more restaurants are open on Thanksgiving than Christmas, and you are more likely to be invited to someone's home if you are new to the area.

You always have the option of volunteering with a group that serves holiday meals. Don't be offended if there is a surplus of volunteers that day and they would appreciate a monetary donation for the food.

RELIGIOUS HOLIDAYS

Religious holidays such as Easter, Passover, Hanukah, Iftar celebrations during Ramadan, and Christmas are generally family-focused. These can be hard for people even when they aren't in a new place. If you're new in town, you may be invited to someone's home, but that's more common for Thanksgiving than religious holidays.

We don't live near family, so lately have spent Christmas without them. My church in Muncie, Indiana had a Christmas noon dinner. The church provided the meat and people came with other food and games. I LOVED that day. In Illinois, one of the Temples has a huge community breakfast, and I see a lot of friends there.

Do you want to create local traditions? These could be for your family or immediate friends, or you could organize something low-key for others. One of the resources noted suggests an online gathering via Skype (Windows or Android) or Face Time (Apple).

RESOURCES FOR CHAPTER SEVEN
Holidays: Do You Stay or Do You Go?

LONLINESS VERSUS BEING ALONE

Part of these two article (and others) address loneliness; other parts discuss things to do when you are alone. The site is terrific for anyone, especially good if you have social anxiety.

How To Cope When You're Alone on Thanksgiving, Arlin Cuncic, on VeryWell Mind, Updated May 2019.
https://www.verywellmind.com/how-to-cope-when-you-are-alone-at-thanksgiving-3024302
How to Cope When You are Alone on Christmas, Arlin Cuncic on VeryWell Mind, Updated March 2019
https://www.verywellmind.com/how-to-cope-when-you-are-alone-at-christmas-3024301

The Holidays Bring Joy As Well As Stress: 10 Ways to Make Them Happy and Avoid the Blues,
Susan Anderson, Huffington Post Life Blog, December 15, 2016
https://www.huffpost.com/entry/the-holidays-bring-joy-as-well-as-stress-10-ways-to-make-them-happy-and-avoid-the-blues_b_8725316

FINDING THINGS TO DO FOR VARIED HOLIDAYS

For any holiday search for "ABC Activities" and local events will appear. These articles might give you some overall ideas.

Fourth of July Activities Are Fun for the Whole Family, Cara J. Stevens on the Family Education Blog
https://www.familyeducation.com/fourth-july/fourth-july-activities-are-fun-whole-family

How to Celebrate Thanksgiving When You're Alone or Away From Home
https://orchidrepublic.com/blogs/news/how-to-celebrate-thanksgiving-when-youre-alone-and-away-from-home

HALLOWEEN

Travel and Leisure Magazine usually had features about Halloween events in different cities.

General Search results
https://www.travelandleisure.com/search?q=halloween

Best U.S. Cites for Halloween
https://www.travelandleisure.com/holiday-travel/halloween/best-cities-halloween-ranking

My former town – Halloween in Washington, DC
https://www.travelandleisure.com/articles/washington-dc-best-things-to-do-halloween

CHAPTER EIGHT
What About Major Life Changes?

You could have moved to be near other family or better medical facilities. Maybe you moved because your spouse died and you're carving a new life in a new place. Picking up this book meant you wanted to thrive in a new place – or someone else wanted to help you do that. I hope you've gotten some good ideas.

What happens if you get to a new place and life circumstances change drastically – you lose your partner or a job, a child you used to live closer to is suddenly ill and you wish you were nearby again, a spouse files for divorce. Life goes on, but you have to adjust.

My husband and I had been in Illinois a couple years when he had a heart attack. We had friendly neighbors (one of whom offered to come to the ER) and I had made friends through church. Still, that first evening I felt more alone than I ever had.

Fortunately the hospital was terrific and the staff paid a lot of attention to my needs, too. We were lucky; and he recovered.

In the midst of a life change you generally have support, but afterwards you go forward with the support systems you put in place.

AFTER THE LOSS OF AN IMPORTANT PERSON IN YOUR LIFE

Experts recommend no major changes, such as a move, for six months to a year after the death of a spouse or partner. Your loss may not involve death, but it could be just as final. Such changes are individual decisions, and vary by many factors.

Loss of a family member is generally known to others in your life, but that may not be the case with death of a close friend. Friends may have been part of your life a lot longer than a spouse. They may not be in your new town, but life will look different without someone you've known for decades.

If you are grieving a pet, don't let anyone tell you "it's not the same" as losing a person. It can be just as sad.

Let's say you decide to stay in your town. No matter how long you've been there, a lot will seem different. Even your friends. Some invite you out or bring food regularly for a while, others aren't sure how to help. You can tell them.

What you can also do is tell yourself it's okay to have sad days and good days, and you can definitely give yourself permission to feel joyful – even laugh. I have several family photos I look at or events I remember when I'm sad. If you remember laughing hard at a movie, rent it.

Then go back to the early chapters of this book and review how to break into a new community. There are things to do that you would not have thought about with your partner or best friend.

If you are uncertain or sad at being on your own you can:

- Plan two or three weekly activities you can do on no set schedule. Go to a fitness club, buy a small order of groceries, visit the library, read a book in a coffee shop, visit the Mall food court. (Watch out for the extra calories. Wait. You can go to the fit club more.)

- Schedule one event or activity that involves you making (and keeping) a commitment.

- Get outside! Even if it's really cold or hot, breathing fresh air can brighten your day.

- Volunteer for an activity or event that is not onerous. If you can't think of one, check the newspaper or online community website for requests. Almost every food pantry needs help stocking shelves – you don't have to agree to do it weekly.

- Buy something new for yourself or to donate to a charity. You don't have to spend a lot of money. Go to a thrift store.

- Read or watch a You Tube video about how to move beyond grief. (See the Resources section.)

I'm not a counselor. If your sadness doesn't begin to lift, ask for help. The hospice that helped us when my dad was dying had a grief support group, as do many hospitals and some churches. The resources section has a couple of ideas.

STAYING IN YOUR NEW TOWN

Criteria for whether to stay in a relatively new place are personal.

- Do you like your apartment or house, and can you easily get around in it?

- Have you made the kind of friends you could call on in an emergency?

- Can you get where you want to go fairly easily? Is there public transportation, can you still drive with comfort?

- Are you close enough to family and friends for them to visit you or vice-versa?

- How happy are you with the medical facilities and your own doctor?

- Do your finances support continuing to live independently (or in your present circumstance, anyway)?

- If you need short-term assistance after an illness or accident, are there people who would help, or a caregiver organization you can afford?

- If you have to transition to assisted living or a nursing home, are there local places you like and can afford?

If your assessment comes up positive, I'm glad you are comfortable in your town. If you don't have family nearby, think about these things.

Many of these apply if you live alone at age 25 or 75.

- How secure is your home? Sometimes local police – or even a smart neighbor – will help you assess locks, window locations, or the need for an alarm system.

- Who will miss you if you don't open the front door in the morning? You need a system to have someone check on you, and you can do the same for them.

- If you go out to shovel snow or sweep the front walk in the winter, who will you tell that you'll be outside for a few minutes?

- How careful are you to ALWAYS have your mobile phone with you? If not, develop the habit. I keep an old one in the car, because even an inactive cell phone will let you dial emergency responders.

- Should you consider a move to a senior apartment or assisted living now, when you can still handle things yourself?

- Did you adjust your will after the death of your partner or spouse?

- Did you adjust your living will after the death of the person to whom you had previously trusted decisions?

- Do you have a list of medications and major health issues in your purse or wallet? You can do it in tiny print so it fits on a small card.

- Have you planned ahead for the next major holiday?

YOU CAN BE ALONE

Most people like having friends around some of the time, but you don't need a new partner or friend in your life to be happy. You will likely be lonely at times, but it won't last forever.

It may sound glib, but it's good to have a gratitude list. Maybe you'll get mad or sad and toss it one day, but you can do another one. If you aren't living on the street, you have things to be thankful for. Having the list helps.

SETBACKS AS OPPORTUNITIES

I'm sorry if you lost a person or a job, and hope you can find a new equilibrium. A close friend of mine lost her husband a few years ago and was convinced that she'd never be truly happy again. A few weeks ago I returned to the town we had lived in concurrently at one point. There she was with her new husband and new group of friends. She is having a ball.

Whether alone or with someone, an activity you began after a loss may bring you hours of joy. Renowned artist Grandma Moses (1860-1961) started painting at age 70. She painted some early work on wood. She got a bunch of orders not long after she started and didn't have enough paintings. She sawed one in half.

Sometimes you just have to look at things differently.

RESOURCES FOR CHAPTER EIGHT
What about Major Life Changes?

The Five Stages of Grief after Losing a Job, on Life Hacker, Kristin Wong, August 20, 2015
https://lifehacker.com/the-five-stages-of-grief-after-losing-a-job-1725201444

10 Things You Can Do to Create a New Life After Any Loss, Kristen Meekhof, Psychology Today, November 11, 2015
https://www.psychologytoday.com/us/blog/widows-guide-healing/201511/10-things-you-can-do-create-new-life-after-any-loss

Grieving the Death of a Spouse, From the HealGrief.org website. There are some excellent references on this site, and your library or local hospital may have more.
https://healgrief.org/grieving-the-death-of-a-spouse

Online grief support group via
https://www.taps.org.
800-959-TAPS (8277)

Lap of Love. Grief Support for loss of a pet. Many resources here.
https://www.lapoflove.com/community/Pet-Loss-Support

**Lots of Resources on Aging –
They Deal with Living and Loss**

Put your fingers on the keyboard and search for national or local groups that can help you manage aging and the changes related to it.

If you want more information on aging (exercise, caregiving, cognitive function), one site that may be helpful is that of the National Institute on Aging. You'll find dozens of helpful links and thoughtful articles.
https://www.nia.nih.gov (click on Health Info)

Look for local umbrella organizations for guidance in your own area. If you aren't sure what to search for, look at these two blogs and search for some of the topics mentioned.

If you live in or near San Francisco, visit the blog of the Institute on Aging (not a federal organization). https://blog.ioaging.org/

Massachusetts has the Healthy Aging Collaborative. Like the San Francisco group, it covers many topics, including links to local groups. https://mahealthyagingcollaborative.org/programs/overview/

CHAPTER NINE
Keeping Those New Friends

One of the hardest things about moving is leaving friends and family.

In Girl Scouts we often sang a song, "Make new friends, but keep the old, one is silver and the other gold." The origin is poem written by Joseph Parry (1841-1903). We authors like to give credit where it's due. I've always assumed the 'old' friends were gold.

I've lived in three neighborhoods (beyond my childhood one) where you could knock on a neighbor's door and visit without an invitation. It didn't mean you could barge in, simply that you were welcome and (if convenient) you could stay to chat.

Those are the places that are hardest to leave.

IN THE REAL WORLD

I think the key to maintaining friendships is a genuine desire to preserve the relationships. Awareness through social media is one thing, visiting is another.

When you're older, real-world connections can be easier in some ways and harder in others. On the one hand, your schedule may be more flexible, allowing for vacations with friends. Even if you still work, you may have been with an employer long enough that there would be no question about you taking time off for the 40th high school reunion.

On the other, travel can be more difficult when you're older. Even if your health is good, a spouse's may not be. There may be more people in your life (sons and daughters-in-law and their families, grandchildren), so it's more complex to schedule weekend getaways. Especially during graduation season.

Some people make fun of holiday season letters, but two pages and a few pictures tell a good story. I keep them for a year or two. Mine rarely make it before New Year's, but I figure my friends have more time to read them after the December rush.

I have a mental list of friends whose spouses' or siblings' funerals I would go to. I think these are more meaningful (for the friend) than going to their funeral. That may not be a very pleasant thought, but it's an important list.

May you see one another many times before you have to attend such events.

ONGOING FRIENDSHIPS THROUGH GROUPS AT A DISTANCE

Some of your hobbies or professional interests can lead you to organizations of others with the same pursuits. Since you will maintain those interests as you move, you may find local chapters.

If you don't, you'll still have the same kinds of distance relationships with people you met through the years in your specialized groups. You saw them periodically before, and that's how you'll see them again.

Do you know anyone who does family history research? It's addictive. Through the years I've developed regular correspondents, and we joyfully share 'finds' and point one another to good sources. I've also made a couple close friends in other states, and we've gotten together.

I know people who belong to national genealogical groups and organize a lot of their free time around the hobby and groups. In fact, almost every library has a genealogy room and/or monthly meeting.

My longest-lasting friendships are through a professional group I joined when I was twenty-six. (For those good at math, that was forty-two years ago.) I was very active in the American Society for Public Administration, locally and nationally.

Even though my writing career has led me to other organizations, I retain a membership and love visiting the friends when I return to DC or go to the occasional national meeting. Letters from these friends are my favorites during the holidays.

Now, I've made friends through Sisters in Crime (which has sister and mister members) and annually attend a conference in Indianapolis (Magna Cum Murder). Lots of familiar people to eat lunch with at these and similar events.

In fact, I was invited to be in a critique group in Decatur, Illinois through people I met at a writing conference. They became my first friends after moving to the state – at age sixty-three.

These kinds of friendships, even if not the best-buddy type, help you feel rooted when your residence migrates because of an unexpected move.

SOCIAL MEDIA AND WEB-BASED CONNECTIONS

In the age of social media you can more easily know what's going on in a friend's life. Some people limit posts about family and friends to close friends, others post broadly. I enjoy keeping up-to-date on friends' lives – births, achievements, career changes. I've reconnected with a few high school and college friends I'd lost touch with.

Online postings are no substitute for personal contact or even phone calls. However, I find the biggest advantage is that I can check on people at odd hours, when I'd never feel free to call.

Future historians won't have access to letter among friends, but that's the price for immediacy, I suppose.

I differentiate between social media and technology such as Facetime and Skype, because video chatting is more like being with someone.

One grandmother I know Face Times with grandchildren almost every night.

Make new friends but keep the old,
one is silver and the other gold.

RESOURCES FOR CHAPTER NINE
Keeping Those New Friends

The Top Five Habits of Friends Who are Good at Staying in Touch, Sam Udotong on Fireflies.ai blog, July 6, 2016.
https://blog.fireflies.ai/top-5-habits-of-friends-that-are-good-at-staying-in-touch-52e8166a60c9

ABOUT THE AUTHOR

Elaine L. Orr primarily writes traditional or cozy mysteries – defined as mysteries without a lot of gore that feature an amateur sleuth. She began writing *Falling Into Place* almost fifteen years before she published it. The story needed to feel just right.

Her Jolie Gentil cozy mystery series has ten books and a prequel. *Behind the Walls* was a finalist for the 2014 Chanticleer Mystery and Mayhem Awards. The first book in her Iowa River's Edge series, *From Newsprint to Footprints*, came out in late 2015, and the Logland series began with *Tip a Hat to Murder* in 2016.

She also writes plays and novellas, including the one-act play, *Common Ground* published in 2015. Her novella, *Biding Time*, was one of five finalists in the National Press Club's first fiction contest, in 1993. Elaine conducts presentations and teaches online classes on book publishing and other writing-related topics. Nonfiction includes *Writing in Retirement: Putting New Year's Resolutions to Work,* and *Words to Write By: Getting Your Thoughts on Paper.*

Elaine grew up in Maryland and moved to the Midwest in 1994. She received her B.A. from the University of Dayton and M.A. from the American University. She did some journalism course work at the University of Maryland and took fiction courses from The Writer's Center in Bethesda, MD, the University of Iowa Summer Writing Festival, and Georgetown University's Continuing Education Program. Elaine is a regular attendee at Magna Cum Murder. She is a member of Sisters in Crime and the Indiana Writers' Center.

OTHER BOOKS BY ELAINE L. ORR

Elaine's books are generally self-published, via Lifelong Dreams Publishing and are at all online retailers. They are available as ebooks, paperbacks, large print, and audio books. Your local bookstore or library can order the books.

Jolie Gentil Cozy Mystery Series
Appraisal for Murder
Rekindling Motives
When the Carny Comes to Town
Any Port in a Storm
Trouble on the Doorstep
Behind the Walls
Vague Images
Ground to a Halt
Holidays in Ocean Alley
The Unexpected Resolution
Jolie and Scoobie High School Misadventures (prequel)

River's Edge Mystery Series (Annie Acorn LLC Publishing)
From Newsprint to Footprints
Demise of a Devious Neighbor
Demise of a Devious Suspect

Logland Mystery Series
Tip a Hat to Murder
Final Cycle
Final Operation

General Fiction
Falling Into Place
Biding Time
In the Shadow of Light

Nonfiction
Monett (Arcadia Publishing)
Writing When Time is Scarce: and Getting the Work Published
Orr, Campbell, Mitchell, Shirley Families: Descendants of Paul Orr and Isabella Boyd in Ireland and America

http://www.elaineorr.com

Check the index on my blog, Irish Roots Author, for articles on reading, writing, publishing, and whatever musings are going through my head.
http://elaineorr.blogspot.com

Whatever you do, enjoy reading!

Made in the USA
Lexington, KY
10 December 2019